DITCH THE SCRUBS

START A
HOME CARE
AGENCY

Your **COMPLETE GUIDE** to leaving bedside nursing
and starting a profitable **HOME CARE AGENCY**

CHRISTINE BACCI

DITCH THE SCRUBS

START A HOME CARE AGENCY

Your **COMPLETE GUIDE** to leaving bedside nursing
and starting a profitable **HOME CARE AGENCY**

Cover design by Ivica Jandrijevic
Interior layout and design by www.writingnights.org
Book preparation by Chad Robertson

ISBN: 978-1-7373323-0-5
Library of Congress Cataloging-in-publication Data:
Names: Bacci, Christine, author
TITLE: Ditch the Scrubs Presents Start a Homecare Agency — Your Complete
Guide to Leaving Bedside Nursing and Starting a
Profitable Home Care Agency / Christine Bacci
Description: Ditch the Scrubs Press, Wichita, Kansas, 2021
IDENTIFIERS: ISBN 978-1-7373323-0-5 (Perfect bound) |
978-1-7373323-1-2 (eBook)
SUBJECTS: | Entrepreneurship | Homecare | Nursing
Classification: Pending
LC record pending

Published by Ditch the Scrubs Press
Printed in the United States of America.
Printed on acid-free paper.

24   23   22   21   8   7   6   5   4   3   2   1

This book is dedicated to all my family with all my love – All that I AM is for you.

'Who am I, Sovereign Lord, and what is my family, that you have brought me this far?' —2 Samuel 7:18

Anything is possible for those
with a DREAM, a PLAN, and the WILL
to make it happen.

CONTENTS

PART III – I JUST RECEIVED MY HOME CARE AGENCY LICENSE. NOW WHAT?

INTRODUCTION

Warren Buffett is famous for quoting, "If you don't find a way to make money while you sleep, you will work until you die," and he is dead right. While nursing is a profession that allows us to care for people in the moments of their greatest needs—fulfilling our own need to care for others—bedside nursing will rarely lead to accumulating wealth. Instead, most nurses will work for 40+ years, earning just enough to be beyond the poverty level, becoming burned out by politics and the wear and tear on their body.

Opening a Home Care agency is one way that you can "earn money while you sleep." It allows you the opportunity to work for yourself without the demands of structured employment, create employment opportunities for others, provide care for those in need, and earn an unlimited amount of money. Essentially, you are able to exponentially increase your earning potential—because you will earn money for every hour someone else goes to work. Sounds like a great idea, right? So why doesn't everyone do it?

For over 20 years, I have met and talked to health care professionals of all levels who have been impressed and marveled at the fact that I was self-employed and owned my own business. They are always curious and ask what they need to do to get their own business started. I have every time provided some basic information, ending with you must do your research and homework. Well, let me tell you now, so few people have moved on to do a thing. The fact that you have bought this book means that you have taken the first crucial step. The first step to change. The first step in your journey to entrepreneurship.

I grew up the oldest of five children in my mother's home. As a first-born child, leadership was an inherent trait. From the time I was a little girl, I was babysitting the younger kids, holding "school" where I was the teacher, selling things to them from my kitchen "store," and generally being the boss. I got my first paying job when I was only 12 years old. I volunteered through our youth group at a department store summer sale called Henry's. While most of the teens were only there to stock the clothing and help customers carry out their purchases, within hours, they had put me on a cash register and taught me how to ring customers up. The following summer, I was offered a paid summer job as a cashier. When I was 18, I convinced my dad to take money out of his 401(k) (neither one of us knew what a bad financial decision that was) to let me start a restaurant with my sister, and we opened Two Sisters Taco Shop. We ran that shop for almost a year.

In 2000, I started LPN school with my sister and graduated 10 months later. Our first job was with a Home Health company that worked with Technology dependent babies under a Medicaid waiver. We both took care of the same ventilator baby for almost three years. Less than two years after graduating as an LPN, I began working acute care rehab in the hospital, learning to use a variety of nursing skills we had learned about in school, whereas my sister went into long-term care and became the administrator of an assisted living. She loved the relaxing pace of the elderly while I was always looking for a challenging fast pace and what I could learn next.

In 2003, a fellow LPN graduate told me about a job she was working at. I will never forget when she called me and said, "Christine, you won't believe this job I just got." She told me that she was hired by an owner who wasn't a nurse but needed a nurse to run her residential care home. She said there were old people living in a regular house that was being run like a nursing home and this lady was getting paid $4,000 for each person to live there. Completely intrigued, I began to research what this type of house was called. I found the state's licensure office and contacted them requesting all the information they had to open my own home. They sent me a huge packet of regulations and information, which I read through and put in a drawer. For about a year, the information was in the back of my mind, but I did nothing with it. Life continued rolling past, I got married and pregnant with my second child. I was working full-time at a nursing home by this time and just bored with the routine of work.

In 2004, I finally stopped procrastinating, wrote my policies and applied for licensure. We took my husband's $10,000 Christmas bonus to find and rent a house and complete the necessary renovations to make it handicap accessible, and opened in March 2005. At that time in my city, there were only about ten other group homes. After opening our door, we had all eight beds filled within six weeks. The success was enough to convince my sister to not return to employment after her maternity leave and to come full-time into the new family business. Six months later, we opened our second home and all the beds were filled before we even started.

Within two years, I started a Home Care agency—focusing on non-medical care and immediately began to fill with new clients. Soon, we realized that your aides/staff will make or break your business and reputation and were searching for a solution to the problem. My mom was the one who said, "Why not start your own school and teach them the way you want them to be taught?" So we did. Bethel House Training Institute was started in 2009 teaching CNA, CMA, and HHA classes for credentialing in Kansas.

In 2010, we built and opened eight new care homes, each licensed to provide care for eight residents. We expanded our school to provide heart-healthy cooking classes, which lead us to find a dynamic and extremely talented up and coming chef. The success of his classes was so huge that we opened a restaurant within our cooking studio—initially only three days per week for lunches. The immediate popularity led us to open for dinners and to expand our space. Eventually, we knew we needed to grow into a full-service restaurant and my husband built a 6,000 sq ft in our downtown area that was open seven days a week for both lunch and dinner. Within our first month of being open, we went from $45,000 a month in sales to $150,000 a month. In 2016, we built and opened an upscale speakeasy bar across the street from the restaurant.

During all this time, all three of our healthcare businesses were open and operating. But then, life happened. I had my 5th baby following a tumultuous pregnancy in 2011. Regulations began to change in our state and Medicaid adopted MCOs (Managed Care Organizations) to run the program in 2012 changing billing requirements for some of our programs. I quickly learned that the restaurant industry was nothing like healthcare—our expected 20-30% profit margins simply did not exist and that a business that could pull a 10% return was a rare unicorn. I learned the hard way that if I did not babysit every penny spent in labor and expenses that we were in the red by the month's end. By the end of year two as a full-service restaurant, our healthcare companies were paying for the losses incurred by the restaurant on a monthly basis. My whole family was working in the restaurant and bar for countless hours each week while our healthcare companies were put on autopilot, receiving minimal attention. I worked on Easter, Mother's Day, and Thanksgiving for six years straight—neglecting priceless family time with my own children.

By September 2016, I was burned out. We were down to less than 40 Home Care clients, one care home, the school was cruising along with two classes each month, and the restaurant and bar were floundering. We were all easily working 80+ hours/week and it was never enough. As a family, we sat down and agreed to do a fast together, giving up meat for 21 days. Even my kids agreed to give up meat and pray with us! By the end of the fast, I had the peace I needed to make the decision to close the restaurant. Not something that came easily, as I was fully aware of the cash flow trap that we were in. I met with our

Chef and told him that we intended to close by 12/31/16 and that he was welcome to take it over—with no purchase required. He looked straight at me and said, "I can't do this by myself." So, the decision was made to sell the restaurant. I can't tell you how much peace I had within my heart and soul over making that decision. We had poured six years into making it work, had some great times and bad times, but the time was at an end and it was one of the best business decisions I have ever made. After a fruitless attempt at finding a buyer, we managed a Hail Mary, finding a buyer the first week of December and closing the deal on 12/28/16—just three days short of closing for good.

Following the close of the restaurant, we went through a period of just coasting through life and recovering from the hustle and bustle. I think there was such an adjustment period of not having to work, work, work from sunup to sundown as was required of the restaurant that we all sat back and took a deep breath. My husband had returned to work in manufacturing engineering about nine months prior, and my sister and I took turns coming into the office to open it or taking a late morning. We closed the bar and listed it for sale, content to wait until we found a buyer that could pay close to the asking price.

I decided that I would never again own and run a business that required so much of me. I wanted something that only operated on a 9–5 schedule, with every evening and weekend off. I wanted to spend much needed and deserved time with my family and kids that continued to grow up each and every day. I looked around at my school and put a small amount of effort into developing an online platform, doubling our class capacity and added a few more teachers. For some reason, I never thought much more of our home health and had no plans for it. I even went so far as to reach out to a friend who owned a small home health agency and told him to come look at our office and see if he wanted to do a shared office space. We had a total of 6,500 sq ft of space for our school and office and I told him that we wouldn't't be any competition since we really weren't doing anything with our home health but letting it drift along with the few clients we still had. Little did I know the plans

God had for me and that He knew so much better than me. I thought my friend was a fool to not take me up on my offer, but he did not and found a different space elsewhere.

By the summer of 2017, I got the itch again and was ready for a new challenge. In reviewing our businesses and the potential growth of each, I chose to focus on our Home Care agency, knowing that we would get paid for every hour that other people went to work. Our state had made changes to the regulations and I set out to update our policies, apply for the new licensure and start working on our Home Care agency. I immediately hired two employees to assist me in November and reexamined our company. At the time, we were down to 20 clients, and by the end of 2017, our Home Care agency had only made $400,000 in revenue for the year and had a weekly payroll of $6,000.

Within 60 days of effort of growing our Home Care agency, we gained 30 new clients. By the end of 2018, we had roughly 110 clients and did $2.2M in revenue. My office staff had grown to four employees and I realized the potential that was developing. Once again, I talked my husband into leaving his profession and coming back to work in the family business. In 2019, we grew to 200 clients, seven office staff, and closed the year at $5,500,000 in revenue—finishing with an 18% profit margin of more than $900,000. As of the writing of this book, we are a month from ending 2020 and have already surpassed last year's revenue—closing October with $6.1M in revenue and expect to close around $8M.

The Home Care industry is ever-changing and growing. Following the current pandemic that our nation is experiencing, I believe that it will continue to evolve at unprecedented rates, as we experience the long-term after-effects of a virus that continues to wreak havoc. At the beginning of the pandemic here in the United States, I sat down with my team and told them I knew this would be a time in history that makes or breaks companies and that I was determined to make history as not only having survived but actually having adapted and thrived. Add to that the fact that the baby-boomer generation is at an age of needing assistance in their homes and you have an industry with unlimited growth potential and an optimum time to claim your stake.

One of the things that drew me to nursing was the fact that there were so many facets to it that it would be impossible for a person to not find a niche that fit them. It is unlimited by age group, demographics, and location. You can use the training to teach, to provide hands on, to become an expert on a single topic, or never leave your home. Such diversity and wealth of options are rare within an industry. The opportunities for entrepreneurship within nursing are absolutely boundless. I see nurses who provide consulting, teaching, merchandising, and leadership. Care homes, schools, and Home Health Agencies are just a few of the many things that a nurse can own, run, and make a profit from.

In 1998, America spent around 36 billion dollars on home healthcare. In 2018, America spent more than 102 billion dollars.[1] Home Care is currently the fastest-growing part of the healthcare economy. As America's elderly population continues to grow, so does the demand for health services that can be provided in the comfort of a patient's home.

The time has never been better for you to start and establish your own Home Care agency. Will there be challenges? Yes. Will it require a lot of work? Absolutely. But there is nothing like hard work where you can reap all of the benefits and in the end, it will be so worth it. You can do anything you set your mind to do. And reading this book is the first step of your next chapter. Congratulations on taking your first step.

---

[1] According to the Office of the Actuary of the Centers for Medicare and Medicaid Services (CMS) in figures published in Health Affairs

CHAPTER 1

HOW DO I KNOW IF THIS IS RIGHT FOR ME?

There has never been a better time to start a business

Thirty years ago, being an entrepreneur was different. Starting and running a business was unchartered territory, and just simply was not for everyone. It wasn't even encouraged. But now, the whole scenario has changed. The barriers to entry into entrepreneurship are lower than ever. You don't need a business degree, investors or even a brick-and-mortar office. You can start your business tomorrow with nothing more than an idea and the internet.

So if you're wondering, "Can I start a business?" let me answer that question for you: regardless of how big you want to grow your dream or idea, there has never been a better time to start your own business. Few industries have seen the explosive growth that Home Care is experiencing right now.

Because times have changed and it is so easy to start a business, there are a lot of people getting into a business that may not be a good fit for running a business. So, let's talk about who should run a business and who shouldn't, so you will have a better idea if it is right for you.

You will be good at running a business if:

1. YOU WANT TO HELP PEOPLE

- If you want to help people in some way—by improving their lives, meeting their needs, and helping to solve a problem in their lives—then running a business might be right for you.

2. YOU WANT TO MAKE MONEY

- There is a huge difference between a hobby and a business. A business will make you money, where a hobby will cost you money. A lot of people start off pursuing a hobby for a business and end up losing a lot of money. If you don't want to make money, running a business is probably not right for you. There is nothing wrong with a hobby or not wanting to make money, you just have to acknowledge what is important for you. There are a lot of ways that you cannot make money if that is not important for you—like volunteering or starting a not for profit, but you should not attempt to run a business if one of your goals is not to make money. While caregiving is about giving back to another, you should not feel bad for wanting to make money. It is impossible for a business to succeed if it does not make money.

3. YOU WANT TO WORK HARD

- There is no way to sugarcoat how much work will be required of you to start and run a business. But if you want it bad enough and are willing to put in the hard work, you can run a business. Too often, people look at successful entrepreneurs and desire a similar lifestyle—they want to travel around the world, a million-dollar home, the best cars, and put their children in the best schools—but they are clueless about the work that was required to achieve that level of success. I can promise you it was only achieved after countless hours of working when everyone else was sleeping, watching TV and being content with their life. The most successful business owners weren't people who inherited a business. They are the ones willing to get knocked down over and over again and still get back up and keep going. They are unwilling to accept a *no*, and willing to search high and low for the knowledge that they did not possess. You don't need a business degree or a lot of money to start your own business, but you will need the tenacity and grit that is deep down in you and a will to refuse to give up when it gets hard. You have to be willing to fight, persist and persevere before you ever even get started.

4. YOU WANT TO START A BUSINESS EVEN BEFORE YOU ARE ACTUALLY READY

- So many people I have met tell me that they want to start their own business and work for themselves, but that they are scared. They are scared of the unknown, they are scared of leaving the security of a guaranteed paycheck at their jobs. They are scared of failure. But you want to know a secret? Even the most successful business owners have the same fears. Did they feel scared when they took that first step or invested the last money they had in their business idea? You bet. But they did it anyway! You see, you must commit to your plan of business ownership before you ever even have a business. Nothing else will work. If you do not wholeheartedly believe in your idea and business plan, no one else will either.

Starting and running a business will always begin and end with you. Even as you grow and add support positions, your attitude and commitment will determine the success of your business and the commitment of your team and employees. Daily, submerge yourself in books that offer support, knowledge, and encouragement for your journey and nothing will be off-limits for you!

Throughout the years, I have tried and failed at many different business ideas. When I was 18, my sister and I had a fast-food restaurant in which my dad invested $10,000. Within a year, we failed and had to close. In 2010, I attempted the restaurant world again and we built and opened a full-service restaurant, investing $250,000 of our own personal cash. Later, we built an upscale bar and spent another $150,000 of our personal cash. By 2016, we sold the restaurant for only $50,000 simply to stop the financial bleeding we were experiencing and sold the bar a year later at a loss. Do I regret any of this? Absolutely not! The experience and knowledge that we gained was priceless and carried over into other businesses that were successful. The point is, I decided to commit to being an entrepreneur in 2004 and have never looked back. *No* and *failure* was never an option. I had a family to support and a lifestyle to maintain. I have always told myself that if one business failed to succeed, I would come up with another. No one can tell you any different!

CHAPTER 2

WHAT IS HOME CARE?

Home Care is known by many names that you may have heard before—Home Health Agency, Home Care Agency, or even Skilled Home Health. All of these names mean the same thing. Healthcare services are provided to a client in the comfort and privacy of their own home. It involves any professional support services that allow a person to continue living in their own home. In-home care services can help someone who is aging and needs assistance to live independently; is managing chronic health conditions; is recovering from a medical procedure; or who has special needs or a disability.

Home healthcare is a growing trend simply because of the nature of our healthcare system. As insurance agencies dictate the care that a hospital is able to bill for, more and more often patients are discharged to their homes before they have fully recovered from complex medical procedures. My mom has often told the story of how when she delivered me vaginally back in 1980, she was allowed to stay and recover at the hospital for a full five days. After she had her next four kids by C-section, her recovery was a 10—14 days inpatient. Nowadays, if you have a vaginal delivery, you can be discharged home in less than 24 hours, and I have heard of women giving birth at 7 am and being discharged by 6 pm the same day!

Have a C-section requiring major abdominal surgery and you are sent home in less than 72 hours—regardless of how you feel.

Today's elders and the physically disabled population are given the option of aging in their own homes with help brought in instead of being forced into nursing homes. Every state's Medicaid program has a Home and Community-Based Services division that administers their waivers—groups that members are assigned to. The focus of these waivers is to keep members in their own homes for as long as possible instead of institutionalized in traditional nursing homes.

When you choose to open a Home Care agency, one of the first choices you need to make is to decide who you will provide care for and what level of care you are willing and able to provide. So let's distinguish the three main types and the type of care that each can provide:

Skilled Home Care Agencies

Also known as Medicare-certified agencies, intermittent skilled care, or visiting nurse services—these agencies have the most complete level of care. They are usually responsible for providing medical care that includes full nursing care and supervision. They specialize in providing short-term physician-directed care designed to help a patient prevent or recover from an illness, injury, or hospital stay.

WHAT TYPE OF SERVICES ARE PROVIDED:

- Short-term nursing services—such as wound care, IV med therapies, vital signs, insulin administration, and patient disease education
- Physical, Occupational, and Speech Therapies
- Medical Social Work
- Home Health Aide Services—usually limited to a one-hour visit that provides assistance with bathing

WHO PAYS FOR THIS SERVICE:
When general qualifications are met—a physician orders the services and a clinical assessment deems them necessary, Home Health Services are paid for by:

- Medicare
- Private Insurance

HOW IS CARE PROVIDED:
Skilled home healthcare has to be prescribed by a doctor. Then, care is provided by specialized team members, mainly RNs, LPNs, and certified Home Health Aides, through visits that last up to an hour on a short-term basis until individual goals are met. Patient care is pre-approved by the insurance company for a specific length of time, generally from 4–8 weeks. Any extension must be renewed.

PROS:
Skilled home healthcare can provide some of the highest reimbursement. The national average per client skilled episode is $3,032.

CONS:
It is definitely a numbers game—Skilled Home Care agencies must always be vigilant with marketing and networking to develop relationships with hospitals and doctors who provide the referrals for care. The average length of stay on skilled home health services is only 32 days. That means that you will have a very high client turnover, requiring a lot of work to continually keep new patients coming in. Recently, the skilled Home Care industry has undergone tremendous legislative changes from the Centers for Medicare and Medicaid placing additional regulation and restrictions on care provided, qualifying conditions, and reimbursement. Lastly, it can be extremely expensive, labor-intensive, and timely to establish the certifications by Medicare necessary to accept Medicare as a payment source. The average cost to start a Medicare Certified agency

is between $150,000–350,000 and can take between 6–18 months.

Private Duty Nursing Care

Private Duty Nursing care provides long-term, hourly nursing care at home for adults or children with chronic illness, injury, or disability. Also known as long-term nursing care, catastrophic care, tracheostomy care, ventilator care, shift nursing, or hourly nursing.

WHAT TYPE OF SERVICES ARE PROVIDED:

- Care for diseases or conditions like TBI (Traumatic Brain Injuries), Spinal Cord Injuries (SCI), ALS, MS
- Ventilator Care
- Tracheostomy Care
- Monitoring Vital Signs
- Administering Medications
- Ostomy/Gastrostomy Care
- Feeding Tube Care
- Catheter Care

WHO PAYS FOR THIS SERVICE:

- Private Pay
- Health Insurance
- Veteran's Benefit
- Workers' Compensation
- Medicaid
- Private pay—direct payment from the person receiving the care

HOW IS CARE PROVIDED:

Private duty nursing care is generally prescribed by a doctor. Care is provided primarily in shifts, up to 24 hours/day, 7 days per week.

Pros:

Clients who start services can stay with a Home Care agency for years. A lot of these services are provided by licensed healthcare providers—RNs, LPNs, and Therapists, which can lead to a higher quality of care and client outcomes.

Cons:

Because the level of care can be advanced, for example, tracheostomy care, you may be required to only staff a client with a licensed nurse or respiratory therapist, leading to increased costs and decreased profit margins. Staff development and training can and should be intensive and can be costly.

Personal Care and Companionship

Known by many names including, non-medical Home Care agency, home health aide services, attendant care services, senior care, homemaker care, assistive care, or companion care—by and far, a non-medical Home Care agency is the easiest to start and maintain.

What Types of Services Are Provided:

- Assistance with self-care, including grooming, bathing, dressing and using the toilet
- Enabling safety at home by assisting with mobility—ambulation, transfer, and fall prevention
- Assistance with meal planning and preparation, light housekeeping, laundry, errands, medication reminders and escorting to appointments
- Companionship and engaging in hobbies and activities
- Supervision for clients with Alzheimer's Disease or dementia

Who Pays for This Service:

- Private Pay
- Long-term Care Insurance
- Health Insurance
- Veteran's Benefits
- Workers' Compensation
- Medicaid—Home and Community Based Waivers

HOW IS CARE PROVIDED:
Personal care and companionship do not need to be prescribed by a doctor. Care is provided on an on-going basis according to a schedule that meets a client's needs, up to 24 hours/day, 7 days/week—including possible live-in care.

PROS:
The easiest of all Home Care agencies to open, non-medical personal care and companionship agencies require minimal cash and licensure requirements to open. They are easily suited for any level of healthcare professional to own and operate—even CNAs. They provide the best longevity of client engagement—you can provide services for a client for 20+ years. Reimbursement is tailored to the pay source and is still very lucrative. This type of agency is an excellent springboard to adding additional services or changing your agency licensure after you have an established client base.

CONS:
You are unable to provide complete care for a client. If a client's needs change and they require skilled services, you will have to ensure that you assist with a referral to an appropriate agency. Liability issues can arise if you or your aides attempt to provide care outside your scope of practice, so it is essential that all of your caregivers are taught what they can and cannot do.

PART I

NUTS AND BOLTS

CHAPTER 3

WHAT YOU NEED TO DO TO GET ESTABLISHED

S o … you've decided to start your own Home Care agency. This chapter will cover some of the first essential steps that you must do.

1. Contact your state Home Care licensing office for your state regulations and requirements for licensure: There is no other step more crucial to your business success than this one. It is impossible to open and run a Home Care business if you do not know the regulations by which you must operate for your particular state. Every state is different and there are different levels to licensure in most states. But a lack of knowledge in this one area will kill any chance of success you can ever have. And believe it or not, this step, above all others is a make or break for any Home Care agency. **Failing to know your licensure regulations inside and out, could not only cause business failure and denial of licensure, but also place your own professional nursing license in jeopardy.** You see, every state says that you have an obligation as a licensed healthcare professional to know the regulations under which you must operate. If you fail to do so, you risk your own professional license, as they could choose to come after you as a nurse or other professional. It can be a violation of the Nurse Practice Act for you to violate state regulations. So, it is imperative that you never operate under assumptions or second-hand information. You must know, for yourself, what the regulations are for your state. These regulations will tell you what care you can provide, who you can admit as a patient, and what standards your caregivers must meet.

This information can be gathered through an internet search for "home care licensure regulations in _____ state," or you can simply call the local licensing office and request a startup packet. You can also head over to www.caredocsystems.com where we have a link to each state's licensure office. Because these regulations vary from state to state, you will need to know those for your particular state—what is applicable in Kansas may not apply in Florida. So be thorough in your research and ask good questions! If I were calling the licensure office in Pennsylvania, I would ask the following, "Hello, my name is Christine. I am interested in starting a new non-medical Home Care agency here in Pennsylvania. Can I please request information on the state licensing and regulatory requirements from you? If you don't mail a packet, can you please provide me with information on where I can find the forms and links? If I have questions about these regulations, who can I speak to or direct them to? I would love a name and number or an email address for someone."

Upon receipt of your regulations, I recommend that you do a complete review of them, marking up the packet with every question that you can think of and then *get answers!* You are not done until you understand everything that is applicable to you and the type of Home Care agency that you would like to operate. While no question is a dumb one, you will get a lot more help if you ask intelligent, informed questions that should you have a minimal foundation of knowledge. When someone asks me a question, it is easy to know if they have any clue of what they are talking about. And I will tell you that I am a lot more motivated to help someone who appears to have helped themselves than someone who comes along and can't be bothered to do some simple research.

2. To Franchise or Not to Franchise ... that is the question

One of the decisions you will need to make is whether to go with a National Franchise or start your own independent company. Being aware of the advantages and potential downsides will help you to make an informed decision.

PROS AND CONS OF INDEPENDENCE

The biggest advantage of being independent is that you control every aspect of your business. You are not restricted by territory, marketing programs, high costs or ever-increasing changes in policy and procedure. You are not limited in pricing to your clients or advertising. In addition, you do not have to share your profits by paying ongoing royalty and marketing expenses to the franchising company.

PROS AND CONS OF FRANCHISING

Franchising benefits people who want to start a Home Care agency but are not confident they can do so on their own because of a lack of experience. Almost all franchises offer dedicated support to the Home Care startup—not to be confused with doing it for you! They can offer training classes and resources to build your skills, whereas independent operators are on their own. Additionally, according to the US Chamber of Commerce, success rates for franchises are greater than 90%, which means they have the lowest failure rate of any kind of business. They also offer some things that may not be available to independent agencies, including, financing, suppliers and training. Franchisees are given a jump start with the national marketing and branding they provide. They offer a tried and true business model you can depend on when making important decisions. The downside is that franchising costs are expensive. Initial costs are often high, whereas the independent Home Care agency can control their startup expenses. With a franchise, you will also have limited territory to offer your services and limited marketing.

Whether it is best to go with a Home Care franchise opportunity or stay independent will have a big impact on how you run your business, how quickly you are able to grow, and your overall chances of success. If you do choose to go with a Home Care franchise opportunity, do your research and compare the different companies that are out there. Look at what they offer and how restrictive their rules are. Make the best choice for your new business.

Now that you have an idea of your state's regulations, the financial startup requirements, and how long the licensure process is, you are ready to move forward with establishing your business plan.

3. Come up with a Name

You will need to decide on the name of your new company. Think bigger than your own name, like the Christine Bacci Home Care Agency and find a name that represents you and your values. Google name ideas or talk to friends and family. Some things to keep in mind when choosing your name:

- How easy is it to pronounce and spell?
- How complicated is it? You should avoid names that have too many parts like 'The Christine Bacci Non-Medical Private Care and Companionship Home Health Agency.' Not only is this absolutely ridiculous, but it will also be hard for anyone to remember and could cause confusion when they are trying to search for you.
- Don't pick a name that could be limiting as your company grows: In the above example, if I later decided to add skilled nursing care, no one would ever know from the title of Non-Medical Private Care and Companionship Home Health Agency.
- Choose a name that conveys meaning: If there is meaning in the name, it will be easier for your customers to remember.
- Conduct a Secretary of State search: In order to make your business official, it will need to be registered in your state through

your state's Secretary of State office. Although there can be multiple businesses in different states with the same name, they cannot be in the same state. Also, if a name is too similar to another existing business, the state secretary may not allow you to register it. So you will need to search to ensure the business name chosen is available in your state. See our website for links to your state's licensure office.

- Get feedback on the name: Make a list of viable options and run them by friends, family and co-workers. This valuable feedback can help narrow down your search.
- Make sure the name sounds good when said out loud: You will be repeating this name over and over. Ensure that it is understandable and easy to spell.

4. Register your business with the IRS and obtain an Employer's Identification Number (EIN): Every business you will need to do work with to start and run a business will require that you have an EIN, also known as a tax ID number. This number uniquely identifies you to the IRS and is commonly used for all other governmental and state regulatory bodies so that your business is a distinct legal entity. You will need this number to register with your state tax office, to open business bank accounts, and to apply for credentialing with your client payment sources—insurance companies and CPAs. You can do this on your own and for free at https://www.irs.gov/businesses/small-businesses-self-employed/employer-id-numbers. I would however recommend that you consult with an attorney or business advisor first, as you will be required to choose what company structure your business will register as—a sole proprietor, partnership, or corporation. ** You will have to register an address at this point—obviously, you do not have an office yet, so it is okay to use your personal address for your business at this time.

5. Register your business name with your state's Secretary of State:

Once you have decided on your name you will need to register and purchase the name for your state so that no one else can claim it. This fee can range from $40–250, depending on your state, but must be done. Some states require that you register online or make you file paper documents through the mail or in person. Some states will also require that you file reports soon after registering depending on your business structure. I recommend that you consult with a business attorney or CPA to ensure you are in compliance and registration is done correctly.

6. Apply for a National Provider Identifier or NPI: An NPI is a Health Insurance and Portability and Accountability Act (HIPPA) administrative standard. It is a unique identification number for covered health care providers, created to improve the efficiency and effectiveness of electronic transmission of health information. When it is time to apply for your state licensure and become credentialed as a provider for insurances, you will be required to provide your NPI number and should always know this number. You can apply for this number at: https://nppes.cms.hhs.gov/#/. You must first register for an account, and then come back to the registration page, login and apply for your NPI number.

CHAPTER 4

POLICIES AND PROCEDURES

N ow that you have read the startup information for your state's licensure requirements, you should have seen that your new licensure hinges on your policies and procedures. In fact, in many states, this is the only thing that stands between you and your new Home Care agency license. The state wants to know that you have developed policies and procedures your agency will follow concerning all aspects of your business that will align with their own regulations.

When I first found out about a residential group home in 2004, the one thing that caused me to procrastinate more than any other was writing my policies and procedures to submit with my application. It took me over six months to get them done. Don't be like me! There are a lot of different options that are available to you for your policies and procedures. You can purchase them already written or you can write them yourself. Whichever option you choose, **you must ensure that they match the regulations for your state.** For example, you cannot have a policy that says you will perform a supervisory visit of your home health aide every 90 days if the state regulations require that you do so every 30 days.

Your policies and procedures should be broken down into several different sections.

1. GOVERNMENT OPERATIONS: Policies in this section should identify the name of your Home Care agency and that your governing body has adopted the attached policies for governance. You should have a policy that names your administrator, back-up administrator and Director of Nursing. I recommend that the policies naming these three key roles contain a single line that you can write the name of the person in that role in. This way, if things change in the future, you can always change and replace the name. You should include your table of contents as well as the date of the policies.

At a minimum, this section should include:

- Governing Body
- Approval of Policies and Procedures
- Policy and Procedures Annual Review and Approval
- Statement of Responsibility – Administrator
- Alternate Administrator
- Job Description – Administrator
- Qualifications – Administrator
- Job Description – Alternate Administrator
- Statement of Responsibility – Director of Nursing
- Job Description – Director of Nursing

2. JOB DESCRIPTIONS: The policies in this section should first address how you will perform employment—what must an employee do to apply for your company. Once they have applied, what will your company now do—you will need to address background checks, reference checks, employee in-service and orientation training. Then you will need to have a job description for

every type of caregiver or employee you will have, providing them with an outline of what your agency expectations are for their role as a caregiver. At a minimum, your policies should include:

- Employee Background Check and offer of provisional employment
- A list of current and prohibited offenses that prevent employment in healthcare in your state
- Applicant Interviews
- Reference Checks
- License and Certification Checks
- Employee Performance Evaluations
- Employee TB Testing
- Employee After Employment and Annual Health Assessment
- Employee Orientation and Continuing Education Requirements
- Personnel Records
- Employment of Personnel under Hourly or Per Visit Contract
- Registered Nurse
- Licensed Practical Nurse
- Personal Services Worker or Non-Medical Caregiver
- Home Health Aide – (Please do not confuse a certified Home Health Aide with a CNA or someone who performs home health care but is not certified)
- Certified Nurse Aide
- Supportive Care Worker

Depending on the type of licensure you are applying for, regardless of whether you intend to offer a service or not, some states require that you address and create policies for Professional Healthcare providers and you may need policies for a:

- Physical Therapist
- Occupational Therapist
- Speech-Language Therapist

- Respiratory Therapist
- Registered Dietician
- Medical Social Worker
- Chaplain

3. CLIENT SERVICES THAT WILL BE PROVIDED: The policies in this section will outline what guidelines you will follow in accepting clients, what needs to be done when a client is accepted, and how you will monitor and oversee the care provided. At a minimum, this section should include:

- Home Care Services – Patient Acceptance
- Skilled Nursing Services – Use of
- Skilled Nursing and other Therapeutic Services for non-waivered clients
- Personal Care Services
- Therapy Services
- Social Services
- Nutrition and Dietary Consultation Services
- Respiratory Services
- Provision of Services
- Supervision of Home Health Aide Services
- Supervision of Non-Medical Personal Service Workers
- On-Call RN
- Clinical Records for Clients
- Release and Disclosure of Information
- Multi-disciplinary Team Liaison with supervising professionals

4. OPERATIONAL POLICIES: This section of your policies and procedures manual should address a variety of issues not mentioned before but that are still essential to compliance with regulatory guidelines. Some examples of policies for this section include:

- Abuse, Neglect and Exploitation

- Patient Bill of Rights
- Grievances
- Home Health Aide Training Program – this will only apply if your state allows your licensed home health agency to teach this course

5. SPECIAL CIRCUMSTANCES OR ADDITIONS: This last section can contain any policies that you have to write in response to changing conditions. For example, due to the COVID-19 Pandemic, our agency was required to write policies addressing pre-work assessments, wearing masks and other PPE, COVID positive clients and employees, etc. In addition, as regulations change or you encounter situations that prompt you to write a policy to address them, you can add them to this section, so that a state surveyor can easily identify new policies from your original policies. You will simply need to ensure that each new policy added is dated.

At a minimum, your agency's policy and procedure manual should be reviewed and updated annually or whenever necessary. You should keep the documentation of the date of this review within the first section titled Governmental Operations. When your state performs their survey of your agency, they will want to see that your policies have been reviewed and renewed.

Every office employee in a management role and responsible for the supervision of other employees, should have a copy of your agency's policy and procedures on hand at all times for their reference and should make it a habit to regularly reference them. After all, they reflect the standards that you will be held accountable for.

A last secret to writing your own policies and procedures that I will let you in on—you can literally take your state's policies and procedures and rewrite them word for word–"It is the policy of Christine's Home Care Agency to ensure that _____."

Remember, you have two options when it comes to your policies and procedures—you can write them yourself, following the state's regulations or you can purchase them. There are several vendors and companies that sell them, including our own caredocs.com. Word to the wise—be sure and check out the quality of what you are paying for and go through each one prior to submission for licensure. I have seen policies that someone has bought before and they were embarrassing and completely inadequate. Know what you are buying!

CHAPTER 5

YOUR APPLICATION FOR LICENSURE

By now, you have taken the time to read your state's particular licensure requirements. You know exactly what it will take to request licensure for your new Home Care agency.

Before you submit your application package, make sure that you have met each and every requirement listed. There is nothing worse than the endless circles and frustration you will cause if you fail to include a required piece of information. It does nothing but delays your business goals—that of obtaining licensure so that you may begin accepting clients.

If they require that you provide proof of insurance, you will need to have obtained this coverage. If they require that you deliver the material in a three-ring binder with labeled sections, you must do so. Failure to do so will only delay your approval. I have heard of licensing staff that come across an application that is missing key elements who will stop all further review and put it at the bottom of their stack of applications. Remember, them requesting a correction of a particular piece is a lot more manageable than if they reject your entire application because it is missing required parts.

Let me address a few other important details that I am often asked that affect this stage of the process:

1. What if I am an LPN and my state requires that I submit the name of the RN that will be the Director of Nursing for my agency, but because I have yet to open, I can't afford to hire a nurse yet? What should I do?

- This is a common concern for someone trying to open a Home Care agency that is not an RN. Whether you are a CNA or an LPN, you will be required to designate an RN who will be your agency nurse. And of course, it would be costly to have to hire and pay an RN for a job that they cannot perform while you wait to become licensed—especially when you don't control how long it will take to actually get your license. Ideally, you will already have a network of other nurses that you know that you could ask to fill this role, but if not, my best advice for this problem is to contract with an RN so that you have a placeholder. I encourage you to reach out to RNs within your network and ask everyone you know for a recommendation and come to an agreement with them to be a placeholder for you. They can do this, even if they don't intend to actually work for you after you receive your agency license. You can also search some of the Home Care groups on Facebook and make a post explaining that you are looking for an RN to fill this role so that you can apply for licensure.

If you do this, I highly advise both you and the RN allowing themselves to be placed on your agency application to make an agreement in WRITING that you both sign. It could simply state that Jane Doe, RN, does accept the job of Agency RN for the purposes of applying for licensure for XYZ Home Care Agency. Jane Doe agrees to provide this service from January 5, 2020 until such time as the agency license is approved. XYZ Home Care agrees that as soon as the state licensure is approved, they will offer long-term employment to Jane Doe, RN, first, but that if Jane Doe, RN, declines, XYZ Home Care must employ a new RN to replace Jane Doe, RN, within 30 days of receiving new licensure. During this time, **NO** clients will be accepted for agency care by XYZ Home Care Agency, until a new RN is employed and accepts responsibility. Within 30 days after licensure, Jane Doe, RN, will notify the state licensure office that they are no longer employed as the agency RN for XYZ Home Care Agency regardless of whether a new agency RN has been employed. It would be a good idea for you to ensure that you have the agreement witnessed or notarized with copies provided to both parties. In addition, I would advise that the Home Care Agency pay the RN a fee for this service and maintain the documentation for this payment, preferably paying by check. It could be $250 or $1,000—it doesn't matter. But the fee shows that a contractual relationship was in effect and that the RN is in fact an employee that was paid for their services.

2. My state requires that I submit an employee file for several positions, but I don't have any employees because my business has not been licensed yet. What should I do?

Again, this is not an uncommon requirement. They want to see how you will maintain your employee files and what elements will be included. They also want to see that you are following the policies and procedures that you have submitted for licensure. You will need to find people who fulfill the required roles and create entire employment files for them following your policies. So if your policies require that you pull an Adult Protective Services background check and call and check three references for each home health aide, you will need to ensure that you have submitted the forms in your employee sample file. You will need real data or a real person.

This requirement will actually set you up for success and cause you to be ahead of the game, because you will gain experience actually gathering the required pieces from the different resources at your disposal. If this is a requirement for you, you are going to need to create or purchase forms to use including your company's application form, your reference and interview forms, pull state and federal employee tax forms, create your health questionnaire and TB Skin test forms—and all other forms you would wish for your employees to review and be held accountable to. This would include attendance and payroll policies, as well as any additional policies unique to your employees and client demographics. Once you have these forms created and in place, have the sample employee complete them, process the application as if you were really going to hire them, including performing background checks and reference checks. Know that you can include yourself as the owner for one of the sample employee files in whatever credential you hold. So if you are an LPN, you may only need to include your RN and one home health aide to round out your sample.

3. Do I have to have an office for my agency to submit my application? What address should I put on my license application?

In order to limit startup expenses and out of an abundance of caution concerning how long it can take from submission of an application to approval, if you want to wait to find an office space for your agency, by all means, wait. It is simply not a required startup expense. I know there are times that an application can sit in the Kansas licensing office for up to a full year and the thought of paying rent for that entire time on a business that you cannot operate is ludicrous and a waste of hard-earned money. When you submit your agency's licensure application, you can submit your home address as your agency's office. In doing so, I recommend that you do find a space within your home that can be dedicated as your personal home office. A place that you can keep all forms and paperwork neatly organized and accessible. You can and should add a separate phone line for this space so that your business already has a number that is preserved just for it and can do so at a minimal cost. (I DO NOT recommend that you use a cell phone for your business phone number. You can list your cell phone under your contact information but not as the business phone line. You need to start practicing professionalism now!) I would encourage you to look into affordable shared office spaces that can be obtained for as little as $100 a month but that provide you with a professional atmosphere and a place for storage of your records and belongings.

Once you are sure that you have everything that is required of you, and have reviewed your checklist thoroughly, you are ready to submit your application for licensing. Some states require a fee to process your application—be sure that it is submitted at the same time as the application. In addition, I encourage you to submit a cashier's check or money order for this fee. I have heard of licensure offices processing the payment 4–5 months after submission when they finally get around to reviewing your packet. And the last thing you need is a check coming through your business or personal account that you have forgotten about that results in overdraft fees or rejection by the bank!

Before you submit your application, **be sure and create a copy of your application and all supporting materials in their entirety!** If they require that you submit it in binder form in a very specific order, create a duplicate application binder for your records. Mail is lost all the time and application packets can be misplaced. Besides, if you are notified about a missing piece of documentation that you know you completed, it will be extremely easy to pull the duplicate and resubmit.

PART II

NOW WE PLAY THE WAITING GAME

One of the first things I will tell you to do while you wait on the approval of your license is to gain all the experience that you can in this industry. Are you currently working in the Home Care industry? If the answer to this question is "No," it's time. It is my opinion that successful business owners know every aspect of their business. If you are working as a hospital nurse right now, get a weekend job seeing Home Care clients. All the book reading in the world will not prepare you for going into a client's home and actually providing care. You should experience the dynamics of home care firsthand—from the administrative and office requirements of hiring and charting to the actual caregiving itself. Experience what it is like as a nurse to have to juggle six different patients with a variety of needs. See firsthand just how much paperwork is involved and required. Learn the lingo or jargon of home care. And above all else—*question everything!* Don't do a single thing if you do not understand the why behind it. Only then can you fully appreciate the arena that you are about to step into. It is this experience, above all else, that will help you tailor your agency and its services.

Learn the good and the bad from the agency you work for—you will know what needs to be done better or you may learn the right way to do something. This experience will help you to know the questions you should be asking and the things you will need to research and form a game plan for. If the Home Care agency you work for struggles to gain clients, ask yourself why and how could you do it better. If they struggle to make payroll or complain about not being paid by insurance companies, ask the why? The things you learn now through this practical experience could save you from having to learn them through trial and error in the future.

CHAPTER 6

BUSINESS PLAN

Now that you have submitted your application for licensure, you are ready to get to work. But you may ask, "How can I get to work, Christine if I don't have a license to accept new clients yet?" Now is the time to get to work learning and developing the systems you will use to run your agency. Now is the time to figure out what company you will use for the internet, not when your license is in hand. Now is the time to figure out what agency software and payroll company you will use, not when you have 10 employees wanting to know when they will get paid. In this chapter, we will address some key things you need to develop a plan of action to address.

You may ask why I waited until now to tell you that you need a business plan. And the answer is simple—the waiting process for a license can take so long that it is always best to get your application submitted as soon as possible. The cost to submit an application is not huge—even if you purchased policies and procedures and paid a lawyer or CPA to file your company registration paperwork—the total investment should be less than $3,000. Nothing that is life or death. Yes, it would suck to lose $3,000 if you decided to not open a Home Care agency after applying for a license, but it's not the end of the world.

However, now is the time to get a plan in place. It is time to research and decide how much money needs to be in your bank account, set a budget so you will know how much money you need, set goals as to how many clients you would like to have, and decide if you will work in your own business. There are many considerations in creating a business plan, but at a minimum, you need to address these issues and be sure that your plan includes:

1. EXECUTIVE SUMMARY – This section should be a concise overview of your business plan. Your goal is to draw readers in so that they want to learn more about your company. This section should include:

- Your business name and location
- The services being offered
- Your mission and vision statements
- The specific purpose of your business plan (to secure investors, to set strategies and goals, etc.)

**It is okay to do this section last or to circle back to parts of it as you work through subsequent sections.

2. COMPANY DESCRIPTION – This section should explain who you are, how you operate and what your goals are. It should feature:

- The legal structure of your company (sole prop, partnership, corp)
- A brief history, the nature of your business and the needs you intend to supply
- An overview of your services and customer base
- A summary of your short- and long-term business goals and how you plan to make a profit

3. SERVICES – Clearly describe what you are selling with a focus on customer benefits. Include details about who will provide care, service costs and the net revenue expected from the sale of these services. Consider adding pictures or diagrams. It should feature:

- A detailed description of your service that emphasizes customer benefits
- An explanation of the market role of your service and its advantage over its competitors
- Information about the service's life cycle
- Relevant copyright or trade secret data
- Research and development ideas that may lead to new services

4. MARKET ANALYSIS – Here you will show your industry knowledge and the results of your research. How many seniors in your area? How many other Home Care agencies are within 30 miles, etc. Present conclusions that are based on thorough research. This section should include:

- A sketch of your target demographic – where you will get your clients from
- An industry description and outlook, including statistics
- A detailed evaluation of your competitors, highlighting their strengths and weaknesses

5. STRATEGY AND IMPLEMENTATION – Summarize your sales and marketing strategy and how you will implement them with an operating plan. Include:

- An explanation of how you will promote your business to your customers and enter the market as a viable alternative to your competitor
- Details about cost, pricing and promotions
- An explanation of how the company will operate, following the

operations cycle – attaining new clients, finding employees, and actually providing the care

- Information on sources of labor and the number of expected employees

6. ORGANIZATION AND MANAGEMENT TEAM – Here you will need to outline your company's organizational structure. Identify owners, management team and Board of Directors if you have one. Include the following:

- An organizational chart with descriptions of departments and key employees
- Information about owners, including their names, percentage of ownership, extent of involvement with the company
- Profiles of your management team – including their names, positions, main responsibilities and past experience
- List any advisors – including attorneys, CPAs, advisors

7. FINANCIAL PLANS AND PROJECTIONS – In this last section, you should consult with a CPA after you have completed market research and set goals for your company. Some of the important financial statements that should be part of your plan are:

- Realistic prospective financial information, including forecasted income statements, balance sheets, cash flow statements and capital expenditure budgets for the next 5 years
- A brief analysis of your financial data

Addressing these topics now will force you to think and strategize and help to prevent foreseeable problems from arising in the future.

CHAPTER 7

WHERE WILL YOU HOUSE YOUR BUSINESS?

s I mentioned briefly in the chapter on submitting your application for licensure, initially, you can plan to run your business from the comfort of your own home office. However, the closer you get to licensure and actually accepting clients, you need to consider making a move to a professional office space.

For one, this will help keep your home a place of peace and privacy. The world is loud enough without inviting anyone else into your sanctuary. When you do open up your agency to accepting clients, you can bet that your home office needs will change and you may not be able to adapt. You will need to be able to answer your business line throughout the day without interruptions or noise from pets and other family members. You will need to occasionally meet with family members outside of the client's home and meet with potential employees for interview and training purposes. You definitely do not want them in your personal space!

Since office space can come at a premium cost, especially depending on where you live, I am a huge fan of shared office space for startups. There are companies who market office space that is complete with a desk, computer and dedicated staff to answer the phone for you with your own company's name—and all for under $100 a month. They usually have shared conference rooms that you can sign up to use, as well as expensive technology that you may not be ready to purchase like large copiers for volume copies. These spaces will also have hugely discounted options to rent a space that is complete as a small office. I remember that our first company office was in one of these shared office spaces. It was called Office This, and I was able to rent a small office with three desks and three computers for only about $500/month which was all that we could afford at the time. It came with all expenses paid, excellent concierge staff that greeted any company's guests, and beautiful conference rooms that you could reserve for no additional charge. It did not take us long to figure out that we talked too loud and too much to be so close to each other and we had to upgrade to the next size up, but it was perfect for us as we got started. There is usually little to no commitment required, making it ideal for when you are just getting started.

Another option to consider is sharing space with another local small business owner that would rent a room in their office to you on a short-term basis.

Some benefits to working from an office:

- Research has shown that face-to-face communication is the most preferred method by employees. It is not only beneficial when planning for a business, but it helps to strengthen relationships and build rapport with people.
- Following a schedule – When working from an office, you are more likely to follow a set schedule. When you work from home, your schedule is much more flexible and can become inconsistent. If you have committed to working on your business four hours each day, but work from home, you can quickly become inconsistent due to the distractions that tend to creep in. While writing this chapter, working from home, I have gotten up to snack, change the laundry and go check on the bathroom that

my 11-year-old son just cleaned. I have answered 10 questions from my other kids and pulled some frozen meat from the freezer. Great for multi-tasking, but inefficient from a working standpoint. I would probably already be done with this chapter if not for the distractions! 😊

Whatever you decide, and whatever your budget, consider making an office space of some kind a priority. The action of actually leaving your home and entering your work "office" will lend itself to increased productivity in the long run and help to establish the professionalism you will need to be successful.

CHAPTER 8

COMMUNICATION

Remember back in Chapter 5 when I talked about the phone number to list for the company on your licensure application? I'd like to take a minute and talk about your need for communication in your business.

If you listened to me, you already established a business phone line. These can be obtained for under $25/month and can follow you anywhere. If you started in a home office and later move to a professional office space, you can even have your number transferred to the new location for little to no cost. Most phone companies will do so at no cost to you. You will need this number and should always use it when completing any forms or registration for your business. Please do not make the mistake of passing out your personal cell phone number to the insurance companies you will be signing up with or to potential clients or employees! Protect your peace! You know how you already don't like to answer your cell phone when a number pops up that you don't know. Well in business, every number that pops up—whether from a prospective employee or client—you won't know. And guess what? You better answer each and every one of them if you want to run a successful agency. So don't start off on the wrong foot by giving your personal cell phone number or you will regret it later.

When filling out paperwork for your business, always give your business phone line. If you are able to distinguish yourself from the business and want to list an additional contact number, then you can use your cell phone—but otherwise, stick to the standard of only giving your business number out. It is better for a potential business client to have to leave a message on your business line because you were not at your desk than for you to answer your cell phone with a mean, "What!" All because you thought it was a personal call.

If you must be away from your office line for an extended period of time, take the time to learn the functions of your service. You should be able to easily forward calls to the number of your choice for a short period of time—ensuring you don't miss any important calls.

Consider getting a company cell phone line. I have done this several different ways, but in the end, decided that I prefer to have a separate phone that I carry around knowing that I must be professional every time I answer it. I know that some carriers offer digital lines that they can install on your existing phone that will prevent you from having to carry a second phone around. We have found through experience that the lines work well, but there are missing options that we found essential. For example, with our digital lines, my staffers can take turns having on-call by simply activating a button on an app they have installed on their phones. But, we have found the digital lines do not allow you to save a name to a contact, and they do not have audible notifications for when you receive a text message and a lot of our employees like to text.

In addition to a dedicated business phone, the closer you get to opening or printing marketing materials, you will need to purchase a second dedicated phone line to use for a fax machine. If you have never operated a fax machine, it is time to learn. Fax machines are essential to Home Care operations. We routinely receive client care plans, authorizations, medical records, and even employee timesheets by fax on a daily basis. And because of HIPPA laws, even if you rent a shared office space, you will have to have your own dedicated fax machine to protect any confidential information you may receive. You can get a quality machine for under

$200, but this should definitely be an early investment.

Lastly, you will need a professional business email. Too often, I see new companies display an email address of XYZHomecare@gmail.com. Aside from being unprofessional, these generic public email hosts are not private and could put you in jeopardy of having your clients' confidential information hacked. There are several options available to you that will offer you not only a professional appearance, but also the security that you will need. Google Business Suites offers business email accounts that start at around $12/month. Sites like GoDaddy and Microsoft Office 365 offer business accounts for even cheaper. My personal favorite to work with is Gmail and I have found the fee worth the convenience of ample storage and how user-friendly it is. In order to set up your business email, you will need to purchase your domain name or dot.com name first, which is covered in the next chapter.

CHAPTER 9
ADVERTISING AND MARKETING

I t is never too early to think about marketing for your company. While waiting for licensure, you may not be able to actively advertise to find clients, but there are so many elements to advertising and marketing that NOW is the time to think about them to help you form a plan for when you can actually get started. Review these marketing ideas, strategize and form your plan now.

1. PURCHASE YOUR DOMAIN NAME AND CREATE AN INFORMATIVE WEBSITE – Although you might think the elderly are not tech-savvy, you better believe that their kids and grandkids that will probably make a lot of decisions are. Now is the time to invest in creating your online presence. The first place people search for information is online, and the first marketing tool you will need to have ready is your website. It does not need to be fancy and expensive, but it does need to be professional and informative. It is the first way you will ensure your potential clients that you are legit and trustworthy. You can spend less than $250 on a well-designed simple website that speaks volumes for you, by using local services or some of the contract artists on sites like Fiverr or Upwork.

2. CREATE A BRAND IDENTITY – Regardless of the size of your agency, you must create a brand identity. Your logo, slogan, and business card are an important part of your brand identity that helps to create an impression with your clients and generate trust. Now is the time to have your logo designed, as you will want to ensure that you incorporate it in every aspect of your marketing—from your business cards to brochures you leave with companies and potential clients, to company business forms. Doing this now will save you the trouble of having to alter materials later.

3. CREATE A STRONG SOCIAL MEDIA PRESENCE – You can create a Facebook business page before you ever even accept your first client. This will allow you time to create content and gather files you will want to share later. Your FB page will sit inactive until you are ready to publish it and send out invitations for others to join. Consider other social media platforms like Instagram and Twitter and set up your sites. Look into services that offer informative and engaging content that is already prepared and written.

4. ATTEND, SPONSOR AND PARTICIPATE IN COMMUNITY EVENTS – Consider organizing or taking part in a community service project or event. This helps to provide visibility, establishes your brand as service-oriented, and allows you the opportunity to network and meet other healthcare professionals you may work with in the future as well as potential clients and caregivers.

5. CREATE A GOOGLE MY BUSINESS PROFILE – Doing this allows you to manage how your information appears across various Google services, including Google search results and Google Maps

6. VOLUNTEER TO SPEAK AT SENIOR-RELATED COMMUNITY EVENTS – Many communities have a variety of senior-related events and welcome speakers. This is a good opportunity to build awareness and trust in your company and brand. However, do take the time to ensure that you are offering valuable insights to the event and not just taking advantage of the free opportunity to market your company.

7. JOIN LOCAL BUSINESS ORGANIZATIONS – Not only do they provide the opportunity for you to meet and network with other like-minded business professionals, but they can also offer some valuable education and opportunities that you should be taking advantage of. Local organizations can be resources of invaluable information for the Home Care agency owner and can be a source of experience, advice, knowledge and skills that entrepreneurs often share. Even if there is not another Home Care agency present, you can learn things that help with other aspects of your business like changing employer regulations, tax law changes, and information on how local politics affect your business industry. Check into membership with your local SBA office, SCORE and Chamber of Commerce in your area, and any other local industry associations available. Furthermore, I highly encourage you to find and join multiple Home Care groups on Facebook. There are a plethora of groups available that all encourage networking and sharing of ideas and resources. Be careful of some of the advice you read and definitely always do your own research before applying a new idea to your business. But they are easily an incredible referral source on industry changes, ideas to solve common problems that all Home Care agencies face, services being offered such as payroll and company management software, and someone to lend an ear that may be experiencing some of the very same issues as you.

8. CREATE A STRONG REFERRAL PROGRAM – Your Home Care agency will thrive with referrals and word of mouth advertising. You should have a special referral program with incentives already thought out. For professional referral sources, you might consider financial incentives whereas for client referrals you may choose to offer free or discounted services, for example, refer a new client that signs up and receive 10 free hours of personal care.

CHAPTER 10
BUSINESS ESSENTIALS

A nother area that deserves mentioning is various business essentials you are going to need to put thought and effort into before you ever accept your first client for care.

CLIENT MEDICAL RECORDS – Even if you are a non-medical Home Care agency, you are going to be required to maintain a client file for every new client. At a minimum, this file should include admission paperwork like acceptance of your agency's policies on billing, cancellations, and emergencies; essential contact information like Name, DOB, Address, Social Security Number, insurance information, power of attorney information and their physician's information. Additionally, you will need a form for your nurse to use to document a visit and assessment, and a form to create a plan of care for your caregivers to follow. What will these forms look like for your agency? It is a good idea to create a checklist of what you expect to have in each and every client's files as well as to create a sample file. This way when you actually have clients, you will not miss important details.

You should refer to the policies and procedures manual that you created that addressed what would be included in your client records and ensure that you have the form in hand for each designation. You can create these yourself—there are many examples of forms that you can find with a simple google search or you can purchase them. But you will want to ensure that they are consistent in appearance, match your company's brand by identifying them with your logo or company name, and that they are available for use. You can't wait until after you already have clients to design a form for documenting the care provided. While our agency uses Home Care software and does upload some of our medical records, we still maintain a paper file folder for each client. We love the medical record style—5 expanding sections with two prongs. They handle very well and fit nice and neat in a regular file cabinet. They can be found on Amazon.

HOME CARE MANAGEMENT SOFTWARE – Take this opportunity to do your research on web platforms that help you manage and oversee your agency. One of my biggest regrets is doing pen and paper and excel worksheets that did not talk to each other for way too many years when there was a wide variety of management software out there. I convinced myself that my system was working and that I had no time or need to learn new software. Boy, was I wrong! We had not been using our new software for more than a month when it was immediately apparent how much easier our lives were becoming. We immediately saw results and were able to implement necessary changes simply because we were able to track data in real-time. The cost of the program was quickly dwarfed by the gains we experienced both in the income we earned and in our office staff's productivity. You can get excellent reviews and referrals from the Home Care groups on Facebook by simply searching the group files, narrow down your search and start doing research to figure out which program will benefit you most. You can contact the companies and request a demo of their program and should be able to make an informed choice concerning a system that will be in place when you accept your first client. This will enable you time to learn to navigate the program and get your forms loaded and ready for use.

Another reason I encourage new agency owners to adopt a management program as soon as possible is because a lot of the built-in features will help you to identify needs that you didn't even know you had. Some come with capabilities that support onboarding employees, provide you with forms to use for different services, provide payroll support or a timekeeping system. This is the perfect time to explore all of the options that are available to you, helping to ensure that you run your business as efficiently as possible from the first day.

BOOKKEEPING AND PAYROLL – Should you try to manage these things yourself or hire them out? Now is the time to decide. I recommend that you start with a visit or consultation with a local CPA who has experience with small business owners. They can be a source of incredible information on your options you will need to make these choices. I will warn you—as a new agency owner, your plate will be filled with the day-to-day operations of running your agency. From finding new clients and employees to ensuring compliance with regulations, you will have plenty to fill your time. If you do decide to manage your own bookkeeping and payroll in-house, know that your already full to-do list could be stretched too thin to sustain long-term and that it could end up being more costly to fix mistakes that could have been avoided.

From the time that I was 12, I had learned to do my parents' annual tax return. It was fairly simple as we were a middle-class income family with no assets. But I allowed the experience to foolishly convince me that I had no need to pay a professional to manage my taxes and that I knew what I was doing—even after starting my own business. Fast forward five years in business and one day an IRS agent showed up at my door. My heart dropped as I met with him and had to admit that I had not been accountable to my business financial obligations and had accumulated a $500,000 tax debt from the failure to file and pay my employer payroll taxes. By the time they were done calculating penalties and interest—and doing their special kind of math that seems to magically multiple simple figures to three, four and even five times the starting number—the balance I owed them was over a million dollars! How foolish I had been! It was a hard lesson to learn and one that I want you to avoid. If there is no other expense to be saved, paying a professional to maintain accurate financial and payroll records is absolutely essential! They will ensure you are in compliance with state and federal tax laws and can hold you accountable to your budget and income restrictions. One of the worst mistakes any Home Care agency owner can make is to start spending the money that comes in as revenue or cash flow thinking it is your profit—a choice that will eventually lead to your financial demise.

PART III

I JUST RECEIVED MY HOME CARE AGENCY LICENSE.

NOW WHAT?

CHAPTER 11

DIVERSIFY YOUR CHOICES AND OPPORTUNITIES – PAYMENT SOURCES EXPLAINED

Now that you have a Home Care agency license and can begin to accept new clients, we need to discuss the different payment sources for your clients. You need to be familiar with the different sources as some require that you register and complete a process of credentialing that is similar to what you just went through to become licensed. Because there are so many different Home Care agencies that you compete with for clients, you will need to increase your chances for success by ensuring that you have more than one source for accepting clients. Too often, a client's choice of provider is limited to who will accept their payment source and not who is the best man for the job. Clients with Medicaid can only choose a Home Care agency that is an approved Medicaid provider, just like a client with Medicare can only choose a Medicare Certified Agency to provide their care, not their daughter's friend.

Private Pay

Clients that come with the means to pay out of pocket for their own care are what we call private pay. They can choose the provider of their choice that fits the budget they have. Depending on the depth of those pockets, they may choose to limit their care to only a few hours a day to make it last or go all out and request 24-hour live-in support. Many Home Care agencies seek private pay clients above all others or choose to only accept private pay clients—the choice is yours.

PROS – Upfront deposits are excellent for cash flow for a startup business. They can afford your highest hourly rate.

CONS – Can potentially be demanding and entitled—they know what they are paying for services and expect to receive every penny of value for their dollar spent. Failure to deliver top-notch service can cause them to move their care to another agency with little to no notice. If you experience a call-off by staff, you will be required to find a replacement worker or as I have heard from many agencies, the owner will go and work the shift themselves to prevent losing the client. If you do choose to only accept private pay clients, you could lose a long-term relationship if and when they run out of money and have to move to state assistance.

Medicare

Original Medicare does not cover non-medical home care aides and only selectively covers home health care. Therefore, assistance for non-medical care is not covered. However, if home health care is considered medically necessary, they will cover it. Visits tend to be brief and procedural in nature and the average length of authorization for a client is less than 30 days. In order to accept Medicare payment for services, a Home Care agency will need to undergo additional credentialing and approvals and must become a Medicare Certified agency.

PROS: Some of the highest reimbursements for procedural services.

CONS: Clients tend to be very short-term in admission, and a Medicare agency will always need to be marketing to secure new clients. The expense of becoming a Medicare Certified Agency can be extremely costly in terms of money and time required.

Medicaid

An insurance program for low-income persons, pays for non-medical care, skilled nursing home healthcare, and other in-home supports to help individuals remain living in their homes. It provides in-home services through a program called Home and Community Based Services, or HCBS. HCBS can be covered under the following:

- Regular Medicaid, often called State Plan Medicaid
- Medicaid Waivers, also called HCBS Waivers
- Community First Choice Option, or CFCO, a relatively new state plan program

State plan Medicaid or regular Medicaid is an entitlement program. This means that if you meet the eligibility requirements, you are able to receive the services. However, waivers are not entitlements. A limited number of slots are available and members will commonly encounter waiting lists for Medicaid waiver services.

PROS: Clients on the HCBS waiver lists must choose an approved Medicaid provider and in some areas the list is small. You can easily increase your client base by accepting Medicaid waivers. Clients on the waiver are told that they must have a backup plan in place if a caregiver is unable to provide them with a worker, so staffing for these clients can be a little less demanding than for private pay clients. Waiver clients are also usually limited on how and why they can change providers, whereas private pay clients can change providers on a whim. You also have little to no marketing expense or effort for Medicaid clients as care coordinators will actively seek you out to accept clients on their roster in need of care.

CONS: Reimbursement is limited—the average is $14–19/hour in many states, but it is a source of guaranteed payment. Low-income clients can present unique challenges for staffing to Home Care agencies—including poor living conditions, pests, mental illness, and alcohol and drug abuse. Your Home Care agency will need to develop a plan to address these issues as they arise.

I recommend that any new Home Care agency keep this option open and available to you. Upon receiving your license, take the time to explore becoming a Medicaid provider and submit the necessary documents. If private pay clients are slow to come along, you can always accept Medicaid clients to fill in the gaps and generate needed revenue.

Veterans Benefits

There are several different forms of assistance that help veterans to afford home care. There are three different pension benefits (cash assistance) that can be applied to the cost of home care. Individuals that require more care can qualify for a higher benefit amount. These are the Improved Pension, Housebound, and Aid and Attendance. Veterans also have the option to receive assistance through a new program called Veterans HCBS. In addition, there is a VA respite care program as well.

PROS:

CONS: Becoming an approved VA provider can be a complicated and lengthy process. There have also been reports of payment delays with processing and receipt of payment.

Long-Term Care Insurance

Some clients have long-term care insurance benefits. This is an insurance policy that pays a flat rate per day for home care. Each client's policy is different and the benefits will vary according to the policy terms.

Some plans will reimburse seniors and some will pay care providers directly. Most plans require that a professional service take place to receive the benefit. For example, a family will not be reimbursed for providing the care unless they are signed up under a licensed Home Care agency. There is no way to pre-sign up with LTC insurers. Rather, when you sign a new client that has LTC insurance as their payor, you will simply need to complete a small amount of paperwork and submit a copy of your state license to activate the benefit or reimbursement for the client.

PROS: A guaranteed payment source that allows your client to meet your private pay Home Care rates. Very simple and short process to become an approved provider, although you cannot do so until you have a client. Your approval is attached to the client, not your agency license.

CONS: They are not a referral source. A common misconception by new agency owners is that they need to get signed up as a provider for LTC insurance and that the agency will send them clients. They do not provide any referrals but instead let their beneficiaries choose their own providers. Beware—most policies have an elimination period at the start of care and the client may or may not understand what this means. This is a period of time after the policy becomes active before the client is eligible for any benefits. Typically, this period is 20–100 days but could be longer. Ensure that your client has met this period or understands that during this period, they will be required to pay out of pocket to cover all services provided.

Although the goal of all Home Care agencies is to have as many private pay clients as possible, understand that a willingness to diversify is key to long-term success. Apply to be credentialed to as many payment sources as possible, take the time to learn and understand how they work, and allow yourself the chance to experience each different payment source and its dynamics and you will set yourself up for success.

CHAPTER 12

FINDING CLIENTS AND CAREGIVERS

So, you may be wondering which comes first? Do I focus on finding clients so that I have work available for newly hired caregivers, or do I find caregivers and risk losing them to another company because I don't yet have any clients to send them to?

I am here to tell you that you must do both ... and both very carefully. Hiring just enough caregivers to have them ready to go when you have a client is a fine balancing act.

Hiring Caregivers

Recruiting and hiring quality caregivers can and will be one of your hardest challenges. Your caregivers will make or break you. What they do and say and how they appear to your clients represents your company's image. It is vital that you take the time to work and find quality caregivers. After all, you cannot have clients if you do not have caregivers to care for them.

Because the Home Care industry suffers from a relatively high turnover rate, it is vital that you create a recruitment strategy that will limit the amount of turnover you experience while at the same time you build a solid team. Follow these steps to develop your onboarding (hiring) process:

1. GET ORGANIZED. Create simple but detailed job descriptions of your job requirements. Describe your ideal caregiver in your ad and make your expectations clear. If you post a generic ad, you will be flooded with unqualified applicants. It is better to be specific.

2. BRIEFLY DESCRIBE YOUR BENEFITS. Good caregivers know their value. Use words like "Great pay" and "Flexible hours" in any employment ads.

3. DESIGN AN EFFECTIVE ADVERTISING STRATEGY.

- Start with an effective platform to advertise your open positions on. If you took the time to find a Home Care Management program, you know whether your software allows you to place job ads and onboard new employees. If it does not, there are many different programs out there at a low monthly cost. I personally like ApplicantStack, which allows you to create unlimited jobs that can be shared to a variety of social media and job site platforms, and then allows you to onboard an unlimited number of employees from start to finish—all for under $125/month.
- Look out for local events and job fairs that you can participate in. Contact your local Workforce department, and any local CNA training schools. Our school allows local employers to actually come over on the last day of class and present information to a group of students about their company and open positions.
- Use Social Media to reach out to potential applicants where they live. In 2020, in the midst of a Nationwide pandemic, we have found Facebook job postings to be the absolute most fruitful for

our Home Care agency. The job posts enable you to choose exactly what age demographic to advertise to, place pictures or memes in the ad for attention, target a specific geographical area, and set the budget you like. When we have a new client come in from a small town in our state, I can set an ad for about $50 within 30 miles of the area to be shown over 3–4 days, and see an immediate return in applicants who are then directed to our website to apply.

4. SPEND TIME INTERVIEWING APPLICANTS and performing reference checks to find the most competent, compassionate aides. You can learn a lot about a person in only 10 minutes of an interview.

5. MONITOR YOUR RESULTS. You will need to have a procedure and reporting in place to let you know just how your recruiting efforts are working. You need to be able to track the cost per hire, how much time per hire, and the job post response over time.

Your recruitment process should not be carved in stone. It's a starting point. You must be flexible and open to changes in strategy to improve the overall effectiveness.

What Should You Look for in a Good Home Care Aide

- YOU NEED A CAREGIVER THAT IS NOT SQUEAMISH. Your aides will routinely have to deal with clients' smoking, their living environment, cleaning bathrooms and kitchens, and providing personal care. They must know what they are expected to do before they walk in.
- YOU NEED A CAREGIVER THAT IS PHYSICALLY CAPABLE OF MEETING THE DEMANDS OF THE JOB. From moving furniture and items in a house to bending over and transferring a client

alone, they must be physically capable of performing the job. You would not want to send a 5'0" 110 lb. young girl to care for a 6'2" paraplegic man who weighs 250 lbs.

- YOU NEED A CAREGIVER WHO IS EASYGOING. We know of an aide who is the most competent caregiver we have ever hired, capable of walking into any situation and knowing exactly what needed to be done. Family members always loved her. But she has one of the most volatile personalities we have ever encountered. She can go from calm and rational to ready to fight a co-worker in minutes. Unfortunately, despite her good work ethic, she is just a liability that we cannot afford to employ. You need a caregiver who can keep calm and go with the flow—so as not to disrupt your client's home.

- YOU NEED A CAREGIVER WHO IS THERE FOR THE LONG-HAUL. It is best to avoid caregivers who tell you that they are only looking for work in the short term or who have a history of jumping from agency to agency, as you will quickly become another peg on their belt. Clients like consistency in staffing above all else.

Remember, your measure of success as a Home Care agency is not in finding a ton of caregivers, but in the **continuity of your caregiving**. *Caregiver consistency is critical to demonstrating your agency's ability to deliver high-quality, personal care by developing trusting relationships with your clients.*

Finding Clients

The success of your Home Care agency depends on you building your client base. After all, without clients, your business cannot provide its service.

Your first step in finding new clients is to have done some homework on other Home Care agencies in your area. What are their rates, what are their hourly minimums? This is a huge help in determining what you can charge and what your agency staffing policies will be. If you charge too much, you won't get many clients. If you charge too little, you are cheating yourself out of income.

Now you are ready to get out there. Introduce yourself to everyone you know who works with seniors or potential clients.

- Contact senior retirement communities—most of the time, this housing arrangement does not provide caregiving services and they welcome the opportunity to provide their residents with resources. Find out about their community events—like Bingo or the monthly BBQ and offer to bring goodies in exchange for being allowed to distribute your marketing materials.
- Use targeted ads on social media platforms advertising your services. Just like with the job ads, you can create simple advertisements and control the demographic they are presented to, and set the budget for your project. There are no minimums and they are extremely easy to do.
- Focus your marketing on places and organizations that have clients in need of the services that you provide.
- Always track the source of any new clients that call for info on your sources. By tracking how your clients learn about your care services, you will know where to invest your time and money for marketing for future clients.
- Consider where the clients with the most needs come from—not just who sends the most clients. One Assisted Living may only send you clients with minimal needs of less than 10 hours/week, whereas another facility may have clients who routinely need an aide for 40+ hours/week.
- Be consistent in following up with your referral sources, thank them for new business and provide them with regular updates on your agency.

Remember, your marketing doesn't end when you have signed a new client to your agency. Instead, it has only begun. You must:

- LISTEN. As simple as it sounds, you must listen to your clients' needs and expectations to help you adapt your services to their desires and ensure client satisfaction.
- BE TRUSTWORTHY. Your client-agency relationship is built on trust. They are trusting you and your caregivers enough to let you into their home to care for who they value most—their loved ones. You must protect the trust they place in you above all else by ensuring that you are dedicated to providing quality care.
- PROVIDE QUALITY CARE. It all comes down to the quality of care that you actually provide. If your agency can provide the care and compassion that they are looking for, they will be your most valuable referral source.

The top 5 reasons clients choose a particular Home Care agency are:

1. The reputation of the company—they can find this through online reviews and what people have to say about your company.
2. Recommendations by family and friends.
3. The recommendation from a referral source—hospital discharge coordinators, social workers, community property managers, and senior services companies
4. Marketing campaign—they saw an ad that persuaded them to contact you.
5. Your company's name was in a directory they were given or you popped up on the internet when they performed a search for "Home Care."

Knowing these reasons, you must value and protect your reputation before everything else. Understand that potential clients will pick your company based on what others say and think about your services.

My Final Thoughts

Follow up on all leads! When you are first starting out, delaying to return a call or even not answering the phone in the first place could cause you to lose out on a potential client. By the time most families call inquiring about care, they are already in need of care and will go with who can start services the sooner. Your policy should be to answer the phone seven days a week, with reasonable hours on the weekends. Return calls as soon as possible and as you grow more established, consider signing up with an on-call customer service company who will answer the phone and represent your company 24/7.

And back to the original question I asked at the start of this chapter—which comes first—the client or the caregiver? My answer is both. I advise that you have no less than three caregivers already signed up with your agency (onboarded and all necessary paperwork completed) before you ever begin looking for your first client. It can be your girlfriend, a co-worker, or your mama. Someone who understands that you are a startup and is willing to be available when you need them—even if it's short term. This way, when you have your first client, you can begin services asap with this worker as a placeholder if necessary, and change them out with a new hire that is available for the long term. Simply be upfront with your client and let them know that you can begin services immediately with a temporary worker but will replace them with someone that will be consistent and long term as soon as you can. I don't recommend that you make this a matter of practice. But it will certainly tide you over until you receive your first couple of clients.

CHAPTER 13
FINAL NOTES

Congratulations on making it this far! If you followed the steps in this book, you have set the foundation for the next chapter in your journey. Entrepreneurship is a journey that is not for the faint at heart. The journey to being a business owner is deciding that you want control over the outcome of your efforts.

In today's society, we all have to work in order to eat. We are taught from the time we enter school that our lives revolve around the cycle of growing up and learning what we can in school, getting a job that we work at for 40 years, and then finally being able to retire and grow old. Owning your own business challenges every predefined limit that has been placed on you. You have the opportunity for growth in every area of your life—both professionally and personally. You control your future. You control your destiny. You control your earning potential.

The strongest fuel to success in your business journey is having a connection to what you are doing. Regardless of your title, your current role in healthcare revolves around one concept—the care of someone in need. Caregiving by definition is giving back to another. Commit your business to adding value to people's lives and it will succeed.

Understand that the journey of entrepreneurship is a journey that is unique for each business owner. Your agency doesn't have to look like any other. You may not want a $5 Million agency and all the work that entails. You may be satisfied with earning enough to be comfortable, able to enjoy the fruits of your labor and may set a goal of having 25 clients netting $250,000 each year. That's okay. The beauty of your journey is that it's yours.

Once you have opened your agency, come back for more. The next book in this series, *From Plans to Profits - How to Grow your Home Care Agency*, will teach you everything you need to know to not only own a Home Care agency but actually Thrive as a Home Care agency.

I'll leave you with this thought by an unknown author—"If you don't have Big Dreams and Goals, you will end up working for someone who does."

ABOUT THE AUTHOR

Christine Bacci is the founder of Ditch the Scrubs, a movement to encourage fellow health professionals to start their own business and create the future of their dreams. With a passion for sharing her hard-earned wisdom after 20 years of entrepreneurship, Christine is best known for growing their Home Care Agency from $200k in annual revenue to $8 Million in less than 3 years and encouraging and helping other aspiring healthcare entrepreneurs to go from barely surviving to thriving. Running a multi-million dollar family business that includes a Health Career College, Residential Care Homes, and a Home Care Agency, she lives in Wichita, KS with her husband and 5 children. With her husband and sister, a fellow nurse, they bring a wealth of Knowledge to the Ditch the Scrubs series.

NEXT STEPS

Now that you're done with this book, here are some next steps for you.

1. JOIN THE COMMUNITY
Join the Ditch the Scrubs community and get early access to upcoming books. Visit our websites and follow us on social media for additional resources —articles, videos, and events to support your journey.

WEBSITES
www.ditchthescrubs.com

FACEBOOK
Ditch the Scrubs

INSTAGRAM
@Ditchthescrubs

2. SHARE THIS BOOK
Please write a review on Amazon and tell others who you think will enjoy this book. Spreading the word helps to reach new readers, grow this movement and the continued production of similar content.

Please leave us a review. That will help us a great deal.

Also, if you haven't yet read our other titles, now would be a good time to take a look.

https://www.amazon.com/dp/B095Z8FCG7

THANK YOU

www.ingramcontent.com/pod-product-compliance
Lightning Source LLC
Chambersburg PA
CBHW072209270326
41930CB00011B/2588